For You, My
Soul Mate

Blue Mountain Arts®

Best-Selling Titles

Been There, Done That, Doing It Better!
By Natasha Josefowitz

A Daughter Is Life's Greatest Gift

For My Wonderful Mother

Keep Believing in Yourself
and Your Dreams

The Path to Success Is Paved with Positive Thinking
By Wally Amos with Stu Glauberman

The Promises of Marriage

A Son Is Life's Greatest Gift

The Strength of Women

Take Time for You
By M. Butler and D. Mastromarino

Today, I Will...
By James Downton, Jr.

A True Friend
...Is Someone Just like You
By BJ Gallagher

For You, My
Soul Mate

*Loving Messages
to Share with a
Very Special Person*

Douglas Pagels

Blue Mountain Press™
Boulder, Colorado

Library of Congress Control Number: 2009926233
ISBN: 978-1-59842-425-6

▉and Blue Mountain Press are registered in U.S. Patent and Trademark Office.
Certain trademarks are used under license.

Printed in China.
First Printing: 2009

✪ This book is printed on recycled paper.

This book is printed on archival quality, white felt, 110 lb. paper. This paper has been specially produced to be acid free (neutral pH) and contains no groundwood or unbleached pulp. It conforms with the requirements of the American National Standards Institute, Inc., so as to ensure that this book will last and be enjoyed by future generations.

Blue Mountain Arts, Inc.

P.O. Box 4549, Boulder, Colorado 80306

Contents

You're My Soul Mate

I am so glad that you're a part of my life. It is such a privilege — to know you, to share myself with you, and to walk together on the paths that take us in so many beautiful directions.

I had heard of "soul mates" before, but I never knew such a person could exist —

until I met you.

Somehow, out of all the twists and turns our lives could have taken, and out of all the chances we might have missed, it almost seems like we were given a meant-to-be moment — to meet, to get to know each other, and to set the stage for a special togetherness.

When I am with you, I know that I am in the presence of someone who makes my life more complete than I ever dreamed it could be.

I turn to you for trust, and you give it openly. I look to you for inspiration, for answers, and for encouragement, and — not only do you never let me down — you lift my spirits up and take my thoughts to places where my troubles seem so much farther away and my joys feel like they're going to stay in my life forever.

I hope you'll stay forever, too. I feel like you're my soul mate. And I want you to know that my world is reassured by you, my tomorrows need to have you near, so many of my smiles depend on you, and my heart is so thankful that you're here.

Every Time I Say
I Love You...

I'm really trying to say so much more than just those three little words. I'm trying to express so many wonderful feelings about you. I'm trying to say that you mean more to me than anyone else in the world.

I'm trying to let you know that I adore you and that I cherish the time we spend together.

I'm trying to explain that I want
you and that I need you and that
I get lost in wonderful thoughts
every time I think about you.

And each time I whisper "I love
you," I'm trying to remind you
that you're the nicest thing that
has ever happened to me.

In Every Way

If I were to make a list of all the things I like most about my life, here's what it would say:

The things I like the most are...
The days I spend with you.
The incredible closeness I enjoy with you.
The conversations I have with you.
The intimacy I share with you.
And the future I want with you.

It's pretty easy to see...
everything ends "with you."
That's how it's been since I met you,
and that's how I know it will always be.

In every way imaginable, you are the one
who completes me.

You're the One
I Want to Be with,
Now and Forever

"I love you with all my heart."

I don't think I'll ever be able to say that enough. It's a feeling that goes with me everywhere I go, and it's one that always makes me smile inside.

You really are the best thing that ever happened to me. I never would have imagined that I could be this happy. I wouldn't have guessed that I'd feel so fulfilled or that I would be so sure of where I want my life to go.

But now I know. I want to be with you. Wherever the journey takes us, I want us to go there hand in hand.

I hope we will be best friends always and kindred spirits through all the seasons to come. I really believe you and I are soul mates and that people as lucky, as loving, and as blessed as we are should always stay together.

There are things in my life that I'm not always clear about... but here are three things I know for sure...

You're the person I want to be with, this is the relationship I want to be in, and ours is the love I want to last forever.

If You Could

If you could see yourself reflected in my eyes, you would see someone who makes my heart just smile inside. You would catch a glimpse of somebody who has been such a wonderful influence on my life and who keeps on making a beautiful difference in my days.

If you could hear the words I would love to share, you would be able to listen to a special tribute to you, one that sings your praises and speaks of an unending gratitude and describes how much I'll always appreciate you.

If you could imagine one of the nicest gifts anyone could ever receive, you would begin to understand what your presence in my life has meant to me.

A Loving Note
About the Person
I Want to Be for You

I want to be so many things for you. I want to be someone who reminds you every single day how much you're loved. I want to be someone who makes you happy.

I want to be someone you can trust with absolutely everything: every feeling you feel like sharing, every hope and worry, every joy, every sorrow. I want to be the one person in the universe you know you can always turn to.

I want to be someone you can laugh with whenever you want to, cry with if you ever need to, and just be yourself with... anytime. I want to be the one thing you're sure about.

I want to be someone who makes you smile a million times more than I make you frown. I want to make beautiful memories with you. I want to go so many places with you. I want to see more sunsets with you than I could even begin to count.

I want to sit across from you at dinner. I want to talk about the day. I want to hold you and walk with you and say a quiet thanks for you as many times as I possibly can... in my time on this earth.

I want to be a part of your tomorrows. I want you to be a part of every one of mine.

And more than anything else, I want to be what you think of every time you think of happiness and devotion and love.

I Keep Falling in Love with You

I am unbelievably lucky to have you in my life.

I think the sweetest thing that can happen to anyone is to meet that one special person who makes you feel like you're living in a dream come true.

That's what this is like for me. It's like that with every smile, every touch, every memory we make.

When almost every day we have together is the kind you don't want to end... that's when you know. That's when love is real, and it's when you realize what a treasure you're holding on to.

Every time we're together, just doing all the things that lovers and best friends and dreamers do, I keep falling in love with you... over and over again.

I could spend forever doing this... and I hope you know how thankful I am for all the incredibly precious things you bring to my life.

A Lasting Reminder

I know I say "I love you!" lots of times, but it's usually as I'm walking out the door and running late for whatever is on the calendar.

But today, maybe I can slow time down a little bit... and tell you how precious that love really is and how much you mean to me. My heart is so grateful for you — for the bond we share, the hopes we have, and the many things we've been blessed with.

I consider the day I fell in love with you — and the moment I knew that you loved me, too — to be the best day my world has ever known.

I have absolutely cherished the times we have had together. Nothing compares with the joy you bring me, the feelings you inspire, or the days just spent side by side and hand in hand... quietly understanding that what we have been given is a gift that will continue to bless our lives.

Even though our everyday world can get too busy for us to say the special things as often as we should, I know, deep within my heart, that what makes life worth living are the things that come to us through our love, our friendship, and our faith in what lies ahead.

I want to tell you all these things in a way that will allow you to hold on to them forever. And if you could ever use a reminder of how much I admire and love and appreciate you, maybe these words can help me say that I truly do... with all my heart.

I Know What a Gift You Are

*You are my very own, one perfect person.
You are everything I always hoped for...
my secret dream that swept me off my feet
and really did come true.*

You have the warmth of the morning sun in your spirit, and you have a gentle soul that I always want to be close to. I deeply, dearly, and happily love you!

I can barely begin to tell you how much I value the exquisite closeness that we have been given. It is a truly beautiful blessing.

There will never be a day when I will take even one moment of that joy and that sweetness for granted. I know what a gift you are.

I want you to know it, too.

*You have an amazing way of touching
my heart, and you have a way of turning
every day into a time and a place where
the nicest feelings and the deepest gratitude
all come together.*

*I have such an immense amount of thanks
and appreciation for all this.*

*And if it's okay with you... I'd love to go
on loving you for the rest of my life.*

What Do I Want in a Relationship?

I want emotional closeness. I want sharing. I want a beautiful bridge between us that is always there, always open, always secure, always ours alone.

I want communication. I want words that speak our language.

I want touches that say more than words can mean. I want to talk things over, whether they're little or large. I want to be more in touch with you than I've ever been before.

I want the things we do to turn into some of the nicest memories any two people could ever ask for.

With you, I want friendship. I want love.
I want gentleness. I want strength. I
want as much happiness as tomorrow
can promise to anyone.

I want to be home to you. I want you to
be home to me.

And I want to be in a relationship that
keeps on growing and goes on giving
the best it has to give.

I found what I was searching for. And now, the thing I most want to do is let you know how very much... I love you.

The Wonders of Love

There are few miracles in this universe as amazing as love. When it is true and real and lasting, it forms an unbreakable bond between two very fortunate people. It is always there and always caring.

Love lives in the deepest part of the heart, but it appears as often as it can... to inspire a grin on the face, a smile in the eyes, a serenity in the soul, and a quiet gratitude in the days.

So Touched by You

Inside of me there is a place... where my sweetest dreams reside, where my highest hopes are kept alive, where my deepest feelings are felt, and where my favorite memories are tucked away, safe and warm.

*My heart is a lasting source of happiness.
Only the most special things in my world
get to come inside and stay there forever.*

*And every time I get in touch with the
hopes, feelings, and memories in my
heart, I realize how deeply my life has
been touched by you.*

You Have So Many Things No One Else Will Ever Have

You have all my love. You have my admiration — for being such an incredibly precious person. You have my unending gratitude — for the way you brighten my life. You have my hopes — all gently hoping you know how glad I am that you warmed my world and touched my very soul.

You have my every affection. You have my desires and dreams. You even have things there are no words for. You have whispered words that belong to you, thoughts you have inspired, and blessings that have touched the deepest part of my heart.

You have empty pages in the story of your life — pages I'd like us to write together... filling them with memories we'll make and stories that will travel beside us and carry us over whatever comes along.

You have my sweet appreciation — for taking my smiles places that my heart has only dreamed of.

And you have the most beautiful wishes the stars and I can wish and my prayer that someday I'll be able to thank you for all this.

Thank You for
All These Things

The nicest feelings I've ever known come from being in love with you.

And I want to thank you for these feelings.

For bringing me happiness as though it were a gift I could open every day... I thank you.

For listening to all the words I want to be able to say... I appreciate you.

For letting me share the most personal parts of your world and for welcoming me with your eyes... I am grateful to you.

For being the wonderful, kind, giving person you are... I admire you.

For being the most beautiful light in my life... I desire you.

For being everything you are to me and for doing it all so beautifully... I love you.

What Is Love?

Love is a wonderful gift. It's a present so precious that words can barely begin to describe it. Love is a feeling, the deepest and sweetest of all. It's incredibly strong and amazingly gentle at the very same time. It is a blessing that should be counted every day. It is nourishment for the soul.

It is a devotion, constantly letting each person know how supportive its certainty can be. Love is a heart filled with affection for the most important person in one's life. Love is looking at the special someone who makes your world go around and absolutely loving what you see.

Love gives meaning to one's world and magic to a million hopes and dreams. It makes the morning shine brighter and each season seem like the nicest anyone ever had.

Love is an invaluable bond that enriches every good thing in life. It gives each hug a tenderness, each heart a happiness, each spirit a steady supply of hope.

Love is an invisible connection that is
exquisitely felt by those who know and
celebrate the joy, warmth, and sweetness
of this gift.

Thoughts and Reflections

I find that you're on my mind more often than any other thought. Sometimes I bring you there purposely... to console me, to warm me, or just to make my day a little brighter.

So often you surprise me, though, and find your own way into my thoughts.

There are times when I awaken and realize what a tender part of my dreams you have been.

And on into the day, whenever a peaceful moment seems to come my way and my imagination is free to run, it takes me running into your arms and allows me to linger there... knowing there's nothing I'd rather do.

I know that my thoughts are only reflecting the loving hopes of my heart... because whenever they wander, they always take me to you.

I Love Having You in My Life

You are such a joy to me! You're the sweet, amazing soul who gave me the chance to experience the kind of love I'd always dreamed of.

Nothing feels more natural than having you here. Sometimes I have the magical feeling I've known you all my life.

I never imagined that loving someone as much as I love you was possible. But if I've learned anything about you... it's that you manage to make special things happen all the time.

And if there is really such a thing as a soul mate... you are definitely
   (and very thankfully!)
      mine.

I Will Always Love You

I am going to love you all of my life, through whatever comes along.

I want us to rise above the obstacles that cause others to separate. I want us to always remember the beautiful things that brought us together.

I want us to look forward to all the tomorrows that are out there, just waiting for us. I want us to have every bit of faith it takes to know that we really can make this turn out right.

I really think that you and I have an opportunity to be as happy as any two people could ever be. That's why this is what I would wish for if I could ask for just one request...

Please... just keep on loving me.

Because no matter what comes along, if we just keep our love strong, we can always work out all the rest.

A Special Promise

There are a thousand things I would like to be for you... but one of the most important is just being someone you can talk to.

There are so many things I would like to do for you and so many things I would like to say and give and share.

It would take me a lifetime to list all the reasons why you are so important to me.

It would take me forever to find words for all the thanks I would like to express... for all the deeply reassuring feelings I have felt in your acceptance of me.

But for now, I just want you to know that in addition to all the love I can possibly give, I promise to be your friend for as long as I live.

I'll always be there, and I'll always care.

I'm Going to Be Here for You, No Matter What

When you need someone to turn to, I'll be here for you. I will do whatever it takes and give as much as I can... to help you find your smile and get you back on steady ground again.

When you just need to talk, I will listen with my heart. And I will do my best to hear the things you may want to say, but can't quite find the words for.

I will never betray the trust you put in me. All I will do is keep on caring and doing my best to see you through. If there are decisions to be made, I may offer a direction to go in. If there are tears to be dried, I will tenderly dry them.

I want you to feel completely at ease about reaching out to me. And don't ever forget this: you couldn't impose on me if you tried. It simply isn't possible.

Your happiness and peace of mind are so closely interwoven with mine that they are inseparable. I will truly, deeply, and completely care about you every day.

You can count on that.

I hope it will invite a little more serenity into your life to know you're not alone, and I hope it will encourage a brighter day to shine through.

I'm not going anywhere. I promise.

Unless it's to come to your side and to hold out a hand... to you.

Will Love Last?

One of the most valuable lessons we can learn from life is this:

Try as we might, we will never have all the answers. We can wonder for the rest of our days whether we are doing the right thing... continuing in the best relationship and following the best paths toward tomorrow, but no one is ever going to answer those questions for us.

We both may have wonderings of what to do and curiosities of what's to come. Time will help us with the results, but more than any one thing, it's up to us — and to the love we have for each other — to go in the right direction.

You and I might sometimes wonder
about where we're headed and
whether our love will last a lifetime.

We may not know the answer, but I'll tell you the one thing I do know:

There's no one I'd rather try to spend forever with... than you.

Nothing Could Be Sweeter Than This

My favorite thing in the entire universe is... just to be sitting across from you, looking into your eyes, talking about anything and everything, and feeling so wonderful inside.

But it's more than that...

It's also holding your hand and walking anywhere the afternoon takes us. It's laughing so easily and trusting so completely.

It's watching the sun go down and the stars come into view and just feeling that, in the grand scheme of things, nothing could possibly be sweeter than having you here...

It's closing my eyes and looking forward to all the joys tomorrow will bring... and thinking about so many different things, like sharing a home, being the happiest family, and making the best memories anyone has ever made.

*It's living our daily lives as two individuals
and dealing with all the demands of the day,
but always finding a hug to come home to.*

*It's cuddling up close. It's feeling so good
and knowing that what we have is so right...*

It's two hearts that are a million times happier together than they could ever be alone.

It's turning a fantasy and a wish into a "happily ever after" dream that has become such a sweet reality.

*It's having a favorite place in the world
and knowing that it's... wherever I am
as long as I'm with you.*

A Little Love Story About You and Me

Me: So lucky to have this special connection!

You: The wonderful person I'm so thankful for.

Me: Someone who means well, but doesn't always get it right.

You: Someone who gives my life so many smiles and so much encouragement.

Me: A little insecure, a little uncertain, a little crazy sometimes.

You: A huge help and a calming influence all the time.

You: Know what's going on inside me better than anyone.

Me: There isn't anybody else I can trust like this and no one I feel so comfortable turning to.

You: On a scale of 1 to 10, with 10 being the best, at least a 20.

Me: Counting my blessings and hearing your name come up so many times.

*You: A joy to be with, to think of, to love
with all my heart, and just to talk to.*

Me: So incredibly glad there's you.

So Many Things
to Smile About

In the time that we have been together, you have made my sun rise on so many mornings — and I'm sure it was you who made my stars come out at night.

You've surprised me with the gifts of hope and laughter and love, and you've made me a believer in the notion that dreams really can come true.

If there are times when you look at me and see my eyes filled with smiles that seem to be reflecting so much love and gratitude, it's because my heart is so full of happiness and because...

*my life is so thankful...
for you.*

About the Author

Best-selling author and editor Douglas Pagels has inspired millions of readers with his insights and his anthologies. No one is better at touching on so many subjects that are deeply personal and truly universal at the same time.

His writings have been translated into over a dozen languages due to their global appeal and inspiring outlook on life, and his work has been quoted by many worthy causes and charitable organizations.

He and his wife live in Colorado, and they are the parents of children in college and beyond. Over the years, Doug has spent much of his time as a classroom volunteer, a youth basketball coach, an advocate for local environmental issues, a frequent traveler, and a craftsman, building a cabin in the Rocky Mountains.